more Photo Fun

Exciting New Ideas for Printing on Fabric for Quilts & Crafts

The Hewlett-Packard Company **with Cyndy Lyle Rymer and Lynn Koolish**

C&T PUBLISHING

Text and Artwork © 2005 C&T Publishing

Publisher: Amy Marson

Editorial Director: Gailen Runge

Acquisitions Editor: Jan Grigsby

HP Technical Director: Joe Hesch

Editors: Cyndy Lyle Rymer, Lynn Koolish

Copyeditor/Proofreader: Wordfirm, Inc.

Cover Designer: Kristen Yenche

Book Designer: Maureen Forys, Happenstance Type-O-Rama

Production Assistant: Kerry Graham

Photography: Luke Mulks, Diane Pedersen, Matt Allen, Kristyn Falkenstern (Hewlett-Packard Company), Lynn Koolish, Cyndy Lyle Rymer; stock photography used throughout courtesy of Photospin.com

Published by C&T Publishing, Inc., P.O. Box 1456, Lafayette, CA 94549

Front cover: Photo by Diane Pedersen

Back cover: *Flower Power* (detail) by Kathleen Brown; *First Marathon in Honolulu* by Cyndy Lyle Rymer; *Peaceful Valley* panorama photo by Lynn Koolish, quilt by Barbara Baker

Attention Teachers: C&T Publishing, Inc., encourages you to use this book as a text for teaching. Contact us at 800-284-1114 or www.ctpub.com for more information about the C&T Teachers Program.

We have taken great care to ensure that the information included in this book is accurate and presented in good faith, but no warranty is provided nor results guaranteed. Having no control over the choices of materials or procedures used, neither the author nor C&T Publishing, Inc., shall have any liability to any person or entity with respect to any loss or damage caused directly or indirectly by the information contained in this book. For your convenience, we post an up-to-date listing of corrections on our website (www.ctpub.com). If a correction is not already noted, please contact our customer service department at ctinfo@ctpub.com or at P.O. Box 1456, Lafayette, CA 94549.

Trademark (™) names, registered trademark (®) names, and copyrighted (c) software products are used throughout this book. Rather than use the symbols with every occurrence of a trademark name, registered trademark name, or copyrighted software product, we are using the names and products only in the editorial fashion and to the benefit of the owner, with no intention of infringement.

Library of Congress Cataloging-in-Publication Data

More photo fun : exciting new ideas for printing on fabric for quilts & crafts / the Hewlett-Packard Company ; with Cyndy Lyle Rymer and Lynn Koolish.

    p. cm.

 Includes index.

 ISBN 1-57120-313-3 (paper trade)

1. Transfer-printing. 2. Photographs on cloth. 3. Textile printing. I. Rymer, Cyndy Lyle, 1955- II. Koolish, Lynn. III. Hewlett-Packard Company.

TT852.7.M67 2005

  746.6'2—dc22

2004029934

Printed in China

10 9 8 7 6 5 4 3

Contents

Acknowledgments

A big thank you to all the companies that provided supplies and information for this book (see Resources on page 63).

Special thanks to Joe Hesch of Hewlett-Packard for his technical know-how and support, to Deb Jungkind of Hewlett-Packard for her enthusiasm and creativity, and to Lori Dvir-Djerassi of Color Textiles for her generosity in providing products, advice, and encouragement.

Quick Start Guide

Special Effects 101

Have you mastered basic printing on fabric with your inkjet printer, and are you wondering what to try next? Or are you just starting out? This book is full of ideas and inspiration for all levels and interests.

POP ART, *32˝× 42˝, Mark and Laura Peterson*

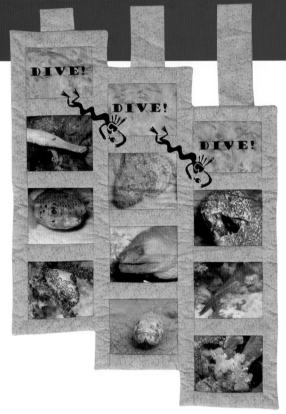

DIVING IN BELIZE, *18˝× 26˝,*
Sue Anderson for Hewlett-Packard

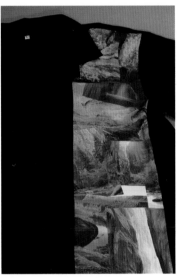

VACATION SHIRT, *Lori*
Dvir-Djerassi for Color Textiles

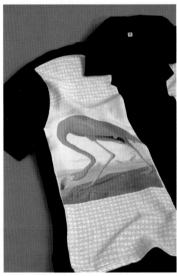

FLAMINGO SHIRT, *Lori*
Dvir-Djerassi for Color Textiles

If you're new to printing on fabric (or you want a quick refresher), check out Back to Basics (starting on page 6) for an overview of the equipment and software we used while creating the effects and examples. We've also included discussions of some of the terminology that's tossed around but not often explained.

If you just have a few questions, check out the Quick Start Guide.

When you're ready, follow the easy Here's How for each effect to create an amazing variety of special effects on fabric. You'll find great ideas for using equipment you may already have—your inkjet printer, an all-in-one printer, a digital camera, or a scanner—and we'll show you all sorts of effects using readily available software programs.

There are many examples and samples throughout for inspiration. Even if you don't sew, there are lots of ideas for quick gifts and home decor. It's all about having fun!

Back to Basics

There are many ways to create the effects presented in this book. Here's a quick overview of the tools and techniques that are commonly used for printing on fabric.

First Things First: Copyright!

Using your own photos and images for printing on fabric is the best guarantee that you own the copyright and, even better, it makes an item uniquely yours.

There are many copyright-free images available in books and online, but if you want to use a photo, drawing, or fabric design created by another person you must ask permission before you use it. Even if you find images on the Internet, you are not allowed to use them unless the website specifically states that the images are copyright-free. Some companies will license images to you for a fee, or you can buy a subscription to a stock photography site such as Photospin.com.

Printers

The one piece of equipment you do need is some type of inkjet printer. You'll be amazed by the quality of the images that can be produced, especially with the newer inkjet printers that are designed to print photos. Plus, almost everyone has an inkjet or knows someone who does.

Printers that handle standard 8½"-wide paper are the norm, but there are printers available that can handle wider paper and fabric sheets. If you have one (or have access to one), they are great to use when you want to print on larger pieces of fabric.

Depending on the type of printer, computer, and software you have, your inkjet printer may do more than you thought it could. The best way to find out is to open a file using any program on your computer, then select *Print* from the program menu bar. When the *Print* screen comes up, you usually have the opportunity to set or change the print *Properties*.

Common print *Properties* include the following:

☐ **Quality:** This property often includes both the quality of the print (from *Draft* or *Fast Print* to *Best*) as well as the type of paper or media (plain paper, photo papers, transparencies, iron-on transfer, greeting cards, etc.). We recommend *Best* for printing on fabric.

☐ **Layout:** Layout options often include the paper size, orientation (*Portrait* or *Landscape*), and *Mirror Image* (see pages 9 and 42–43).

☐ **Features:** Feature options often include *Poster Printing*, *Scale to Page* (enlarge or reduce the image to fit on the given paper size), and *Ink Volume* (this is especially helpful for printing on fabric such as silk, which is more absorbent than cotton, so you might want to reduce the ink volume).

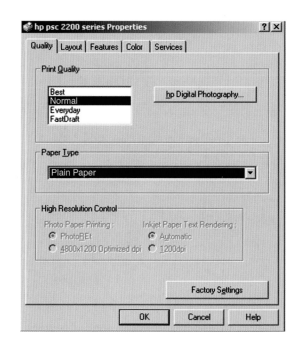

Typical Print Properties; your screen may look different, but will have similar options.

□ **Color:** Options here include printing in *Grayscale* (this is an easy way to change an image from color to black and white) and changing the *Saturation* (see pages 18–19), *Brightness* (see pages 20–21), and *Color tone*.

□ **Paper type:** Many paper types are available, and it is best to set this according to what you are using, but for fabric be sure to select "plain paper." That has produced the best results for us.

The options you have and where they appear will vary, but the information above will give you a good idea of what is often available. You may need to select an *Advanced* option to find some of them. Take a minute to see what your printer can do.

Note The question about printing fabric using a laser printer often comes up. Laser printers should **not** be used for printing on fabric for the following reasons:

□ The fabric backing that is needed to stabilize the fabric will likely jam in the printer.

□ The heat needed for laser printing can permanently bond the treated fabric to the backing. You could also damage the laser printer.

□ The treated fabrics that you make or buy are designed specifically for inkjet inks.

□ There is no guarantee that the toners used in laser printers will permanently adhere to fabric.

ALL-IN-ONE PRINTER/COPIER/SCANNER

An all-in-one printer/copier/scanner is a type of inkjet printer that is easy to use and offers an amazing variety of ways to transform your images. They often have slots for digital camera memory cards. All you do is insert the card from your camera in the appropriate slot, and you can print out a proof sheet of all your photos, select a specific photo to print, or save the photos to your computer. With a Hewlett-Packard All-in-One you can even use the proof sheet to indicate which photos you want to print, then scan the proof sheet, and the printer prints the selected photos in the size and quantity indicated. It doesn't get any easier!

Hewlett-Packard All-in-One

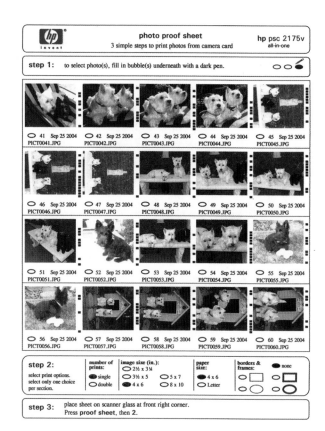

Proof sheets make it easy to choose the photos, including size and quantity, that you want to print from your camera memory card.

Copy or Scan?

You can use an all-in-one as either a copier or a scanner.

□ When you use the copy function, your image is printed directly onto paper or fabric.

□ When you scan, the image is sent to your computer so you can save it on your computer and change it using software, if you like.

You can copy or scan old photos, new photos, drawings, maps, postcards, and any other flat image. You can even create your own beautiful new images by placing 3-D objects on the all-in-one glass bed. Let your imagination take flight, and combine photos with meaningful mementos —the combinations are endless. (See pages 34–35 for more on 3-D scanning and pages 30–31 for more on combining photos and 3-D items.)

When you copy or scan 3-D objects, you can remove the scanner cover (or leave it open) and cover the objects with fabric to block out the light and to provide an interesting background.

3-D scanning with cover open

 Tip When you copy or scan 3-D items that have sharp edges and might scratch the glass scanner or all-in-one bed, place a clear acetate or transparency sheet (available at office supply stores) on the glass to protect it. You can also use plastic wrap, bubble wrap, or other clear or translucent materials to add a layer of color or texture when scanning.

3-D scan with plastic wrap

Both copying and scanning have their advantages; read on to find out more.

Copying

When copying images using newer all-in-ones, you can:

☐ Reduce or enlarge an image, including enlarging to fit to page

☐ Print multiple copies of the same image

☐ Make a poster

☐ Make an image lighter or darker

☐ Change the color intensity

☐ Prepare an iron-on (photo) transfer

☐ Print in black and white rather than color

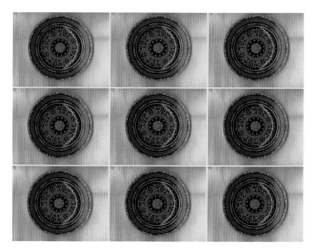

Make multiple copies of the same image. It's a great way to create blocks for a quilt border or for kaleidoscopes (see pages 40–41).

Combine old black-and-white photos and more current photos by printing color photos in black and white.

One of the options that is the most fun to do with an all-in-one is to turn a photo or scanned image into a large poster-size picture by printing it out in 2, 4, 9, 16, or 25 sheets that can be sewn together (see pages 32–33). Add borders created by scanning 3-D objects (see pages 38–39), and you have a one-of-a-kind project.

Scanning

Scanning is as easy as pushing a button. If you don't own an all-in-one or a scanner, your local copier or photo service can scan (digitize) photos for you. Some quilt shops can do this for you for a small fee—check with your quilt shop to see whether it provides this service. Use the largest, highest-quality photos you have available for scanning. Also, scan your photo in the orientation in which it will be used, vertical or horizontal. Some detail is lost when you rotate the photo in your photo-editing or desktop publishing program.

When scanning images, you can

☐ Crop or resize your image

☐ Lighten or darken the image

☐ Sharpen the image

☐ Adjust the color

☐ Change the resolution

☐ Prepare an iron-on (photo) transfer/mirror the images

☐ Invert (reverse) the colors—light becomes dark, and dark becomes light

☐ Mirror the image

Crop *a photo before you scan it.*

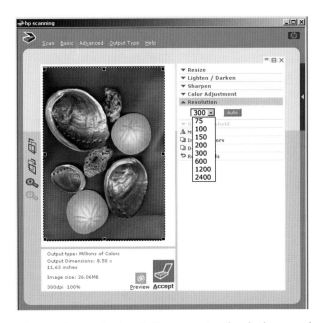

Change the *resolution* before scanning for the best results.

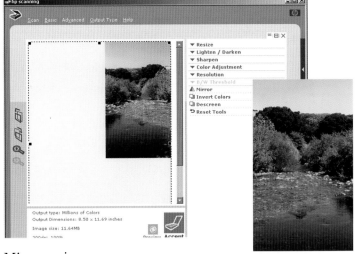

Mirror *an image.*

Original

Tip When you are scanning at a resolution of 300 dpi or higher, make adjustments to the color, saturation, and brightness of your scanned image using photo-editing software, not your scanner software. (See next page for more on dpi and resolution.) Using the scanner software yields good results, but much larger file sizes.

To scan several photos at one time, don't overlap them; leave at least ¼″ on all sides for seam allowance. Before scanning, sort your photos into separate piles based on the size, so you can scan them at the same time. This works especially well when you want to reduce or enlarge several images.

Tip If a glossy photo has fingerprints on it, use a piece of soft flannel to buff them out before scanning.

Storing Digital Images

As you start to acquire more digital images (photos, scans, and so on), you may want to store them on CDs rather than on your hard drive, because they can take up a lot of disk space. You can save images on CD-R (read only) disks—these are less expensive, but you can write to the disk only once. CD-RW (read-write) disks are more expensive, but you can add images to them later.

Digital Camera

A digital camera is not necessary for printing on fabric, but owning a digital camera will greatly expand your creative horizons. In addition, the playback feature lets you see right away if the picture you took is what you want.

Most cameras come with basic photo-editing software that allows you to make significant changes to less-than-perfect photos or to just have fun. You can make colors more muted or more intense, fix red eye, crop, adjust the brightness, and more. You can also save your digital images to a computer, which opens even more doors to photo magic.

In addition to photo-editing software, there is software to create scrapbook pages (see pages 60–62), turn a series of photos into a panorama (see pages 44–45), create a photomontage (see pages 46–47), and more—you'll be amazed at what you can create.

Digital cameras

If you haven't purchased a digital camera or are looking into buying a new one, here are the basic features to look for:

☐ 3–5 megapixel images. The greater the pixel count of an image, the higher the resolution of that image, which in turn results in better-quality images (see next page for more on photo resolution).

☐ Memory cards with 128 to 512 megabytes (MB) or even a gigabyte of storage capacity (you may need to buy an additional memory card with this much storage, but it is well worth it).

☐ Compatibility with your computer. Check the type of connection port: serial, USB, or IR.

☐ AC adapter so you can easily transfer your pictures to your computer without using battery power.

☐ Built-in macro feature that will allow you to focus in close to a subject.

☐ Panorama feature. If you are interested in creating panoramic images, some new cameras have a panorama feature that makes it easy to take pictures that are perfect for joining together into panoramas.

Tip If you're not ready to buy a digital camera, you can now get images from your film camera put on a CD for you. Ask about this option when you drop off your film for processing.

Resolution

Resolution determines the quality of your image—the higher the number, the sharper the final image. Resolution is measured in dots per inch (dpi), which indicates how many dots of ink a printed image contains per square inch of area. If you use a higher resolution, your photo will look its best when printed on fabric. Except for large files such as banners, most of the images in this book are 300 dpi. Higher-resolution images create larger files, so you'll need to balance the resolution with the storage capacity you have. (The greater storage capacity needed is a good reason to start storing your higher-resolution images on CDs.)

What's the Difference Between Megapixels and dpi?

It's easy to become confused when people start talking about megapixels, dpi, and resolution.

Let's start with a *pixel*—it's essentially a dot of color that is stored in either the camera or computer memory. A *megapixel* is 1 million pixels. The more pixels in an image, the clearer (or bigger) the image is when you look at it on your computer.

dpi (dots per inch) is related to printing images and is often referred to as *resolution*. If an image has more *pixels* or *megapixels* when you shoot it, you'll have a higher *dpi* when you print the picture, resulting in a clearer, sharper picture.

Photo printed at 72 dpi

Photo printed at 300 dpi

When you are taking photos, use the largest image size (megapixels) for the sharpest picture, especially if you are planning on printing the image as large as possible. Check your camera manual for image size settings.

When you transfer your images to your computer, don't be surprised if it looks like your images have been transferred at 72 dpi, even though you used the largest image size on your camera. You simply need to use the *Image size / Resize* option in your photo-editing software to change the resolution. Changing the resolution will affect the size of the image, and you can balance the size of the image you want to print and the resolution at which it will print.

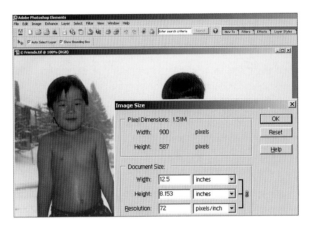

Image from camera at 72 dpi

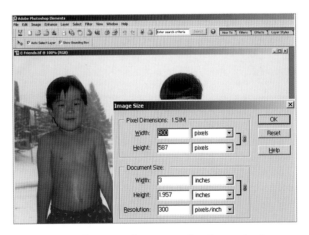

Image resized to 300 dpi; notice the change in the Document Size

> **Tip** If you are scanning photos for a project and plan to use them at a size larger than 4″ × 6″, set the resolution on your scanner to 300 dpi.

Software

There are many types of software programs that can be used when printing images on fabric. For the effects in this book we've used the following:

☐ Photo-editing software

☐ Desktop publishing software, which often includes some photo-editing capabilities

☐ Word-processing software

☐ Specialty software (such as HP's Custom Label Kit and Creative Scrapbook Assistant)

The capabilities of the different types of software often overlap, so your best bet is to become familiar with the software you have to see how you can use it. Many inkjet printers, such as the HP Photosmart printers, come with photo-editing software that is ready to use. Read on to find out more about the different types of software programs.

Most software programs include an online *Help* file. A *Getting Started* option can be particularly helpful if you are using a software program for the first time. Some software programs also include *Hints* or *Recipes* to help you with specific program options.

 Tip Some software makers offer free downloads of trial versions of their software. This is a great way to try a new software product to see whether it meets your needs.

Photo-Editing Software

Photo-editing software gives you the ability to alter your digital images and includes basic editing functions, color adjusting and enhancing, and many types of effects and filters.

The software that comes with your digital camera to transfer images from the camera to the computer usually includes at least basic photo-editing functions. Printers, scanners, and all-in-ones also come with software that may include basic photo editing.

Other software programs are available in various price ranges (or even as free downloads) to perform a variety of functions. The software designed for professionals can be complex, but there are many products available that are designed for the more casual user. Some of the more common brands are Adobe, ArcSoft, and Corel, but any product that works for you is fine to use for printing on fabric.

Desktop publishing software is designed for creating books, newsletters, brochures, cards, and so on. It may include basic photo-editing functions, as well as other capabilities that are perfect for printing on fabric for quilting and other craft projects. Some of the more common brands are Adobe, Broderbund, Corel, Microsoft, and Quark.

Commonly available software

BASIC EDITING

Cropping, resizing, mirroring, rotating, and so on work the same in photo-editing software as they do with printers and scanners (see pages 8–9). You can start the basic editing process with your printer or scanner, but to see what you can really do with photo-editing software, take a look at Cropping (pages 22–23), Reflections and Mirrors (pages 42–43), and Layers and Transparencies (pages 50–51).

Tip Be sure to read page 11 on resolution. You'll get the best results when you understand how the resolution affects the images you are editing.

COLOR

Color can be adjusted to improve a photo or can be taken to extremes for fun and effect. You can make some color adjustments using your printer or scanner, but to see some of the fabulous effects you can create that are related to color, take a look at the following: Saturate It! (pages 18–19), Change Colors (pages 26–27), Adjust Brightness and Contrast (pages 20–21), and Colorize (pages 28–29).

FILTERS AND EFFECTS

Filters and effects are simple ways to alter images in more ways than we can describe. It's as easy as finding the *Filter* or *Effect* menu option in your photo-editing or desktop publishing program and selecting a filter. Individual filters are often in groups such as artistic, blur, sharpen, distort, render, stylize, pixilate, and texture. It's also fun to apply multiple filters to an image and see what happens. If you don't like the effect, just click *Undo*. (See pages 48–49 for much more.)

Original photo   Posterize *filter applied*

Quilters Take Note

Search for a filter or effect option called *Photocopy*, which transforms your photo into a black-and-white outlined image. These images can be used to create patterns for appliqué, redwork (or other embroidery), or for machine- or hand-quilting designs.

Original photo   Photocopy *filter applied*

Terminology varies among the different photo-editing programs. For example, one program may use the term *Filters*, while another uses *Effects*. To change colors or hues, you may need to look under *Enhance, Adjust,* or *Color.* When you start out with a new program, the best approach is to go through a tutorial or just click through all the toolbar menu options to see what's there.

Desktop Publishing Software

We found that desktop publishing software programs provided basic photo-editing capabilities as well as additional options for some of the things we wanted to do for this book, such as printing banners (see pages 36–37) and combining images and text (see pages 24–25). Different programs offer different options. Some of the programs are relatively inexpensive, so you may want to give one a try.

Specialty Software

The best thing about specialty software is that it is designed to perform a specific function and to do it well. We used a few specialty software programs to create some of the effects and examples in this book and were sold on how easy they were to use. When we recommend a specific software program, it's the one we used when creating this book.

For example, the HP Creative Scrapbook Assistant program is designed to create scrapbook pages. We had a blast combining our own images with the images that come with the software, adding text, and creating our own scrapbook "pages" and quilts (see pages 60–62).

Another good example: there are programs that allow you to merge a series of photos together, but none worked as well as a program designed specifically to use multiple images and merge them into a panorama. We used the Panorama Maker software from ArcSoft that came with our HP digital camera, and it merged the photos seamlessly (see pages 44–45).

Our goal in this book is to give you options to achieve effects, but when we found a specific type of software program that worked best, it's the one we chose to use.

HP specialty software

Images on CD

CDs are available that include imagery and project ideas that use the provided images on fabric. You can follow the project instructions or use the images and follow your own ideas. Even though the images are on CD, they may be provided only for your own personal use. Be sure to read the product information so you know what's okay and what's not.

Look for software that offers images and projects.

Getting Ready to Print

So now that you have all your images, you need the fabric to print them on. Fabric needs to be stabilized before you can run it through an inkjet printer. You can prepare your own fabric for printing or purchase pretreated sheets.

PRETREATED FABRIC SHEETS

Many types and brands of pretreated fabric are available at your local quilt store or online. They are washable and ready to use.

☐ You can get pretreated fabric sheets in various sizes: 8½″ × 11″, 8½″ × 14″, 11″ × 17″, and 13″ × 19″. You can also get fabric on rolls that are either 8½″ or 13″ wide. Wider fabric is also available for those with wide-format printers.

☐ A variety of fibers are available: cottons, silks, rayon, and canvas, to name a few. Some manufacturers offer sampler packages that allow you to try different types of fabrics.

☐ You can buy fabric sheets that are designed to be sewn like regular fabric, fabric sheets that are ready to be fused, or "peel-and-stick" sheets that can be used for a wide variety of craft projects.

Many of the manufacturers have websites with product information and lots of project ideas. Check out the resource list on page 63 for website addresses.

Pretreated fabric sheets

Pretreated fabric rolls and large-size sheets

PREPARING YOUR OWN FABRIC SHEETS

You can also prepare your own fabric sheets. It's less expensive and allows for greater creativity. It takes only a few minutes to prepare a few sheets, and you can choose the color and texture of your fabric.

You'll need to treat the fabric with a product to make the inkjet inks permanent and colorfast in the wash. The most commonly used product is Bubble Jet Set 2000 (see Resources on page 63). Regardless of the product used, be sure to follow the manufacturer's instructions.

After the fabric is treated, you need to apply a backing. You can do this by ironing freezer paper or iron-on stabilizer to the back of the fabric or by using 8 ½″ x 11″ adhesive shipping labels. To avoid scorching the fabric, do most of the ironing on the paper, not the fabric. Freezer paper is available in rolls from the grocery store, or you can buy precut freezer-paper sheets designed specifically for ironing to fabric. An alternative backing is full-size laser printer adhesive labels, which are less expensive than inkjet labels and are reusable.

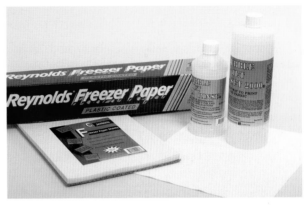

Supplies for making your own treated fabric sheets

Try printing on a variety of fabrics; white-on-white fabrics are fun, and even subtle tone-on-tones work well. Remember that because printers don't print white, any parts of an image that are white in the original will actually appear the same color as your fabric.

Photo printed on patterned fabrics

White fabric gives the truest colors and works great for printing photos. Use 100% cotton with a tight weave, such as pima or kona cotton. Cream-colored muslin adds an aged look to sepia-toned and black-and-white images. Silk works well too.

> **Tip** If you prewash fabric, don't use fabric softener in the washer, or dryer sheets in the dryer. Softener is not needed and may prevent the ink fixative from setting correctly.

OTHER SUPPLIES

Even if your main focus is printing on fabric, you'll want to have some paper supplies. We recommend that you always make a test print on paper before you print on fabric, so in addition to regular printer or copier paper, having banner paper on hand will make your life much easier for banner printing. We also found that when we had great images, we always wanted to print some on photo paper as well as on fabric. For photo transfer, you'll need iron-on photo transfers.

Other supplies

> **Tip** To reduce the potential of jamming, trim the leading corners of your fabric sheets.

Trim corners at 45°.

Printing

Before you print, make sure you know how to feed the fabric sheet into your printer. Does it need to go fabric side up or fabric side down? One way to check is to print on a piece of paper with an ✕ marked on it. Load the paper into the tray with the ✕ face down, and print. If you see the ✕ on the printed page, you've loaded the paper correctly and you need to load your fabric sheets with the fabric face down.

ALWAYS do a test print on paper before printing on fabric. To save ink and time, do test prints using the *Fast* or *Draft* print option.

After you are sure the image is printing correctly, remove all other paper from the paper tray and insert fabric sheets one at a time. If there are any little threads hanging from the sides, trim them with scissors. Check your print options and be sure *Print Quality* is set to *Best* when you are printing on your fabric. Choose the *Plain Paper* option under *Type of Paper*.

> **Tip** Resize photos to a maximum of 8″ × 10½″ so there is seam allowance on all sides.

SUNFLOWER BAG, *16″ × 14″, Jeri Boe*

Bright sunflowers and leaves enliven this tote bag.

Rinsing Prints

In general, after you print on fabric sheets, rinse them one at a time by hand using Bubble Jet Rinse or water to rinse off any excess ink. Dry flat on a towel, and your printed fabric is ready to use—there's no need to heat set it. Fusible and "peel and stick"-type products may not need to be rinsed. Just be sure to follow the instructions on the package of the product you are using.

Tip If you are in a hurry, dry the rinsed sheet with a hair dryer, but never iron the sheets while they are wet or they may scorch.

UP PAJARO-SCOPES, *34″ × 36″, Cyndy Lyle Rymer*

Kaleidoscope Kreator software (see Resources) made it easy to experiment with a variety of photos taken at the beach. Inspiration for the quilt design came from *Thinking Outside the Block* by Sandi Cummings and Karen Flamme.

FLORAL PRIMAVERA, *24″ × 40″, Cyndy Lyle Rymer*

Many close-up shots of spring-time flowers were printed on silk and cotton and fused to a hand-painted grid.

Saturate It!

Why settle for realistic colors when you can change them? Most photo-editing software offers a way to change color saturation. A photo with no color saturation is black and white; a photo with the most saturation is almost day-glo.

Original photo

Saturated photo

What You'll Need

☐ Digital images and photo-editing software

Here's How

PHOTO-EDITING SOFTWARE

Use the software Help tool, Quick Start, Hints, or Recipes as necessary.

1. Open a photo file. Make a copy of the original file by saving the image under a new file name.

2. Look at your software menu options to find *Saturation*. It may appear under a menu item such as *Colors, Enhance, Adjust,* or *Photo Effects* and is often grouped with *Hue*.

3. To tone down an image (or make it black and white), drag the *Saturation* bar down or to the left (depending on your software) or make the level a negative number. To make the image more vibrant, drag the bar up or to the right or make it a positive number.

4. Save your new photo to the new file name.

Typical screen option to adjust the Saturation

Tip If you prefer to scan and then print the image, you may be able to adjust the saturation using the *Print Properties* of your inkjet printer (see pages 6–7).

Tip You can use the *Saturation* option to make a color photo black and white, but some software has an option designed specifically to remove color or convert a photo to sepia tone.

Original photo

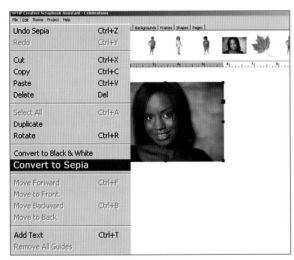

Converted to sepia using HP's Creative Scrapbook Assistant

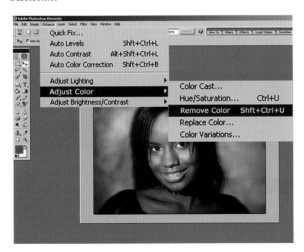

Converted to black and white using Adobe Photoshop Elements

Try This!

☐ Use different levels of *Saturation* on one image to see which level works best for your project.

☐ Make a realistic image abstract by super-saturating it.

Original photo   *Total saturation (+100)*

Make This!

Use your super-saturated printed fabric to dress up a tote or other bag. Printed fabric is also great for adding pockets to the inside or outside of the bag.

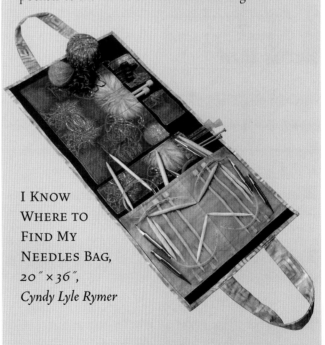

I KNOW WHERE TO FIND MY NEEDLES BAG, *20˝ × 36˝, Cyndy Lyle Rymer*

This needle keeper is made with canvas, fast2fuse double-sided fusible stiff interfacing, and photos printed on broadcloth. Hook-and-loop tape squares keep needles in the pockets. Mirror imaging created an interesting shape with joined needles (see page 42–43).

Adjust Brightness and Contrast

Change the *Brightness* or *Contrast* to make a dull photo dazzling. Fix photos that have a too-bright background or that have details lost in shadows. Or, you can go to extremes and use *Brightness* and *Contrast* to create a totally different look.

Original

Higher Contrast

Maximum Contrast

What You'll Need

☐ Digital images and photo-editing software

Here's How

PHOTO-EDITING SOFTWARE

Use the software Help tool, Quick Start, Hints, or Recipes as necessary.

1. Open a photo file. Make a copy of the original file by saving the image under a new file name.

2. Look at your software menu options to find *Brightness and Contrast*. It may appear under a menu item such as *Colors, Enhance, Adjust,* or *Photo Effects.*

3. Experiment by dragging the slider bars or changing the levels of both *Brightness* and *Contrast* until you are pleased with the image.

4. Save your photo under the new file name.

Use slider bars to adjust Brightness and Contrast.

Try This!

☐ Adjust both *Brightness* and *Contrast* and see how you can change an image.

Original photo

Maximum Contrast (*+100*)

Maximum Contrast (*+100*) *and reduced* Brightness (*-100*)

☐ Combine effects: High contrast and saturated hues, along with some new colors, make an interesting design.

Original photo

Increase Contrast *and* Saturation.

Use a Solarize *filter (see pages 48–49) and increase* Brightness.

Now change the Hue *(see pages 26–27).*

Make This!

This fun, practical bag contains lots of pockets for quilting necessities. The colorful sunset photo glows with increased brightness and contrast.

SUNSET QUILT BAG, *45˝ × 25˝, Beate Nelleman*

Cropping

Cropping and zooming in an image allows you to create a dramatic effect. You can crop and focus in on an element to create an abstract image, create a new focal point, or improve the composition of the image.

Close-up shot of flower

Macro shot of flower

What You'll Need

☐ Camera with macro option
   (that allows extreme close ups) **or**

☐ Printed images and a scanner or all-in-one **or**

☐ Digital images and photo-editing software

Here's How

CAMERA

1. If your camera has a macro option, you can get very close to your subject. Otherwise, get as close to your subject as the camera will allow.

2. Move the camera around to create an interesting composition.

3. Take the picture and use the playback feature of your digital camera to make sure the photo is in focus and you like the image.

SCANNER OR ALL-IN-ONE

1. Choose a photo to work with and place it on the scanner bed.

2. Preview the scan and use the *Crop* function to select the desired portion of the image.

3. You may also be able to *Resize* the image.

4. Scan to your computer.

   (See page 9 for more on cropping while scanning.)

PHOTO-EDITING SOFTWARE

Use the software Help tool, Quick Start, Hints, or Recipes as necessary.

1. Open a photo file. Make a copy of the original file by saving the image under a new file name.

Cropping using software

2. Select the *Crop* tool and use it to frame in and crop the portion of the photo you want to select.

3. Save your new photo under the new file name.

Tip Some programs will let you crop in predefined shapes such as circles and hearts.

Image cropped in a circle using HP's Creative Scrapbook Assistant (see pages 60–62)

Try This!

☐ Focus in on a subject while keeping some background in the picture. When you use the macro option, your subject will be in focus and the background will be blurry, adding depth to the image.

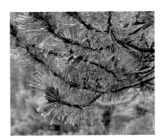

Camera was focused on the pine branch and raindrops and shot with macro option.

☐ Combine cropping with other effects such as Change Colors (pages 26–27), Filters and Effects (pages 48–49), and Saturate It! (pages 18–19).

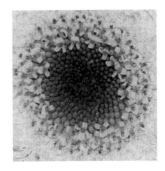

Cropped, recolored flowers

Make This!

Small cropped images can be used in many decorative ways. This tabletop accordion was made by sandwiching fast2fuse double-sided fusible stiff interfacing between two photos for each panel. Wire and beads keep the display together. A layer of Mod Podge was added to heighten the colors and give it even more body.

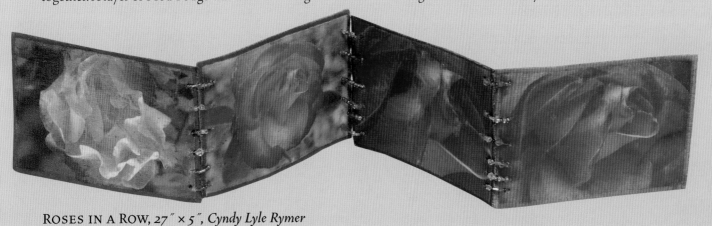

ROSES IN A ROW, *27˝ × 5˝, Cyndy Lyle Rymer*

Add Text

Adding text is a great way to turn your favorite photos into scrapbook pages, make fabric postcards, or to do some personal photojournalism. Add someone's favorite poem to a meaningful photo, and you have an instant gift.

It had been a memorable Mother's Day, sighting a whale, and then being treated to the most glorious sunset...

Text added to a photo using HP's Creative Scrapbook Assistant (see pages 60–62)

Flowers at sunset. What could be more Heavenly?

Using layers is a great way to add text (see pages 50–51).

What You'll Need

☐ Digital images and photo-editing, desktop publishing, word-processing, or specialty software

Here's How

PHOTO-EDITING, DESKTOP PUBLISHING, OR SPECIALTY SOFTWARE

Use the software Help tool, Quick Start, Hints, or Recipes as necessary.

1. Open a photo file. Make a copy of the original file by saving the image under a new file name.

2. Select *Add Text* and type your text in the box. Add *Background* color behind the text (or make it transparent) and adjust the *Size, Color,* and *Font* of the text.

3. Save your image under the new file name.

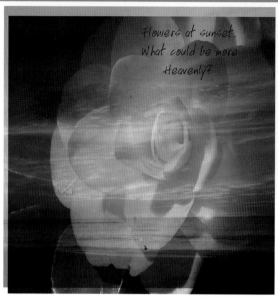

Adding text using HP's Creative Scrapbook Assistant

Tip If you are using photo-editing software and are comfortable using layers (see pages 50–51), you may want to put your text in a separate layer to make it easier to move around.

WORD-PROCESSING SOFTWARE

1. Create a new document, and use *Insert Picture* from the *File* option. Move and resize the photo as necessary.

2. Check the options for combining text and photos. Type in your message, adjusting the *Font, Size,* and *Color.* You can also change the fill and line colors of the box, or select *No Fill* and *No Line.*

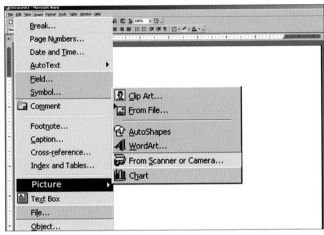

Insert a picture from a file.

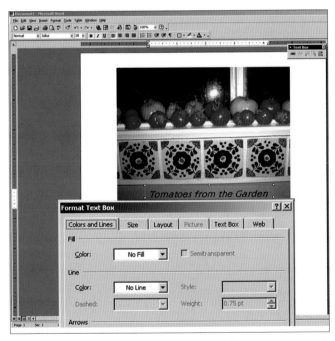

Adjust the Fill *and* Line *colors of the text box.*

3. Save the document.

HAND LETTERING

If you prefer, you can always add hand lettering using fabric markers, fabric paint, or a bleach pen (for dark fabric).

Try This!

☐ Experiment with different font sizes and colors.

☐ Combine text and images to make fabric postcards.

Add shaped text.

Add text and a border.

Make This!

Add text to personalize your projects. A holiday photo is the center of a Log Cabin–style block printed with holiday wishes.

CHRISTMAS PILLOW, *12˝ × 12˝, Katrina Hamer for Hewlett-Packard*

Change Colors

Changing colors (or hues) in a photo is easy to do. You can make subtle changes to improve a photo or radical changes for fun.

Original photo

Color (hue)-adjusted photo

What You'll Need

☐ Digital images and photo-editing software

Here's How

PHOTO-EDITING SOFTWARE

Use the software Help tool, Quick Start, Hints, or Recipes as necessary.

1. Open a photo file. Make a copy of the original file by saving the image under a new file name.

2. Look at your software menu options to find *Hue*. It may appear under a menu item such as *Colors, Enhance, Adjust,* or *Photo Effects* and is often grouped with *Saturation.*

3. Drag the slider bar or adjust the levels until you have the colors you want.

4. When adjusting color/hue, you may also want to adjust *Saturation* (see pages 18–19) and *Lightness.*

5. Save your new photo under the new file name.

✳ ────────────────

Tip In photo-editing terms, changing *color* in a photo is really changing *hue*, not changing a color picture to sepia or black and white. (See page 19 for details on changing a photo from color to either black and white or sepia.)

──────────────── ✳

Try This!

☐ Make a series of images by changing the color/hue of an image many times; combine with other effects.

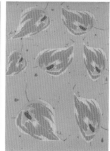

BRIGHTNESS *and* Contrast *were adjusted (see pages 20–21), the image was copied and pasted, then colors/hues were changed.*

☐ Some photo-editing software allows you to select specific colors/hues to adjust within the *Hue/Saturation* option.

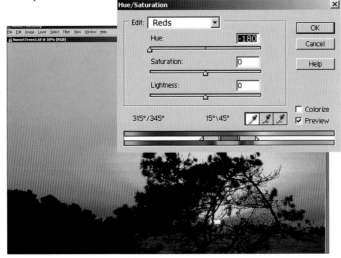

Only red was adjusted in this photo.

✳ ───────────────────────────────

Tip If you are copying or scanning, you can use colored transparency sheets to change the overall color.

─────────────────────────────── ✳

☐ Combine changing colors/hues with other effects such as Cropping (pages 22–23), Filters and Effects (pages 48–49), Saturate It! (pages 18–19), and Adjust Brightness and Contrast (pages 20–21).

☐ Try out different colorways for a quilt by changing colors/hues.

Original quilt   *Colors/hues changed*

Make This!

Quilts are perfect for playing with colors.

It is said that "necessity is the mother of invention." So is not having enough fabric. A small piece of hand-painted fabric was the inspiration for a quilt, but there wasn't enough fabric. It was cut into a heart shape, scanned, and then reproduced in many colors by changing the hue.

HEARTS OF A DIFFERENT COLOR, 22˝ × 21˝, *Lynn Koolish.*

Colorize

Hand coloring black-and-white photos is a time-honored tradition, but now you can do it with photo-editing software. If you don't have photo-editing software, fun and easy ways to change or adjust the colors in your photos are available—break out the art supplies and see what you can do.

Original photo   *Colorized photo*

What You'll Need

☐ Digital images and photo-editing software **or**

☐ Photos and art supplies such as fabric markers, paints, inks, watercolor pencils, and photo pens

Here's How

PHOTO-EDITING SOFTWARE

Use the software Help tool, Quick Start, Hints, or Recipes as necessary.

1. Open a photo file. Make a copy of the original file by saving the image under a new file name. If the photo is in color, convert it to black and white (see page 19).

2. The easiest way to get started is to colorize selected portions of the photo or just the background.

3. Use painting tools such as *Brushes* or the *Paint Bucket* to subtly or dramatically change the original colors of your photo. *Hints* or a program tutorial are good places to start to learn how to use these powerful tools. Select a brush size that is appropriate to the size of the area you are filling.

4. Save your new photo under the new file name.

Tip Using layers is a good way to colorize photos. You can control the transparency of the color, and if you use a new layer for each color, you can delete it if you make a mistake or don't like the way it looks. (See pages 50–51 for more on layers.)

Use a different layer for each color.

HAND COLORIZING

There are two options for manually adding color to a black-and-white or color photo.

1. Color directly on a photo with pens or markers specially made for coloring photos, then copy the painted photo onto fabric.

or

2. Print a photo on fabric, rinse, and let dry. Use fabric inks or paints, fabric markers, or watercolor pencils to add color. Let dry completely before handling.

Use fabric inks, paints, and markers to colorize photos printed on fabric.

Try This!

☐ Use fabric inks or pens to color old black-and-white photos, then copy or scan them to print on fabric.

☐ Colorize portions of a photo.

Only the beret and lips were colored for a vintage effect.

Make This!

Colorized images add a nostalgic touch anywhere they are used. Make a scrapbook or photo album cover by colorizing a favorite old photo, then adding borders.

A black-and-white photo was scanned into the computer, restored, and then "hand" colored on the computer using Photoshop to create the center image. Striped upholstery fabric, buttons, and gold piping make the album cover one that can grace any coffee table, and will be enjoyed for many years to come.

A SALUTE TO DAD, *14˝ × 14˝, Jeri Boe*

Collage

Combining photos, memorabilia, and 3-D objects is a great way to record memorable events. With a scanner or an all-in-one you can place photos and other flat items along with related mementos. Instant collage!

Travel souvenirs collage

Marathon memorabilia collage

What You'll Need

☐ Photos and mementos

☐ Scanner or all-in-one

☐ Clear transparency sheet

Here's How

SCANNER OR ALL-IN-ONE

1. Place a clear acetate or transparency sheet on the bed of your scanner or all-in-one to protect the glass if you are using any 3-D objects that might scratch the glass.

2. Place items face down on the scanner bed. Be sure to place the items you want "in front" first so they are next to the glass. Then layer on the rest of your items.

3. Preview the image and adjust the objects as necessary. Scan.

4. Save the file.

Arrange items on the scanner or printer glass.

Tip Scanning a collage makes it easy to see whether you have everything arranged exactly as you want it. If you want to copy the collage directly onto fabric, make test copies on plain paper in black and white in *Draft* or *Fast print* mode until you are happy with the placement of all your collage materials.

Try This!

☐ Try using different items; you may be surprised at what scans well and what doesn't.

Rubber ducks and bath toys make great images. A baby blanket can be used for a background.

☐ Put tulle or other sheer fabric down first for an interesting texture.

Tulle was placed on scanner bed first.

Make This!

Print a collage and related images on fabric sheets, then sew them together into a scrapbook quilt to commemorate a significant event.

Photos and memorabilia from a first marathon were scanned. HP's Creative Scrapbook Assistant (see pages 60–62) was used to create the title panel on the top of the quilt, then the page was printed using the *Poster* option (see pags 32–33).

FIRST MARATHON IN HONOLULU,
28″ × 72″, Cyndy Lyle Rymer

Make It Poster Size

Is there anything better than taking a great shot and making it bigger? It is so easy to do!

THROUGH A WINDOW, *36″ × 30″, Kathleen Brown for Hewlett-Packard*

What You'll Need

☐ Scanner or all-in-one and a large photo (to keep the quality of the image sharp, use an 8″ × 10″ photo or the largest photo available)

Here's How

ALL-IN-ONE

1. Place the photo face down on the all-in-one bed. In copy mode, choose the *Poster* option and the number of pages.

2. Make test prints on paper to make sure you are pleased with the division of the image; if a seamline falls in a bad place, move the image on the bed, or rotate it 90°.

3. Print on fabric.

Tip For larger seam allowances, with some printers you can use the *Poster Printing* option under *Print Properties*. Be sure to try this on plain paper (and *Fast Draft*) before printing on your fabric.

Tip It's definitely worthwhile to print each piece of a poster-size image on paper before you print on fabric so you can see where the seamlines will fall. Use *draft* mode to save time and ink.

Poor seamline placement

If moving or rotating the photo before copying doesn't result in better seamlines, you can work with the seamlines that divide the photo by very carefully aligning the seams when sewing the sections together. Or you can cut the picture up into sections that will yield a better placement of the seamlines, then enlarge and print each separately on fabric sheets (see Cut It Up on the next page).

CUT IT UP

1. Make a high-quality copy of your image.

2. Cut the copy into the desired number of pieces.

Cut up photo.

Make This!

There are many ways to use poster-size images. You can combine images in interesting patterns and use other effects described in this book.

The images were collaged and text was added. Then the center of the quilt was printed out poster size.

WHITEWATER RAFTING, 40″ × 48″, *Sue Andersen for Hewlett-Packard*

3. Scan or copy and enlarge each piece using the same enlargement percentage for each page.

Enlarge each section.

4. Make test prints on paper, then print each piece onto a separate fabric sheet.

Try This!

☐ Add sashing between pieces to make the image look like a window with panes.

☐ Embellish your poster-size quilt.

SUNNY DAY, 28″ × 26″, *Jennifer Nobile, for Pollards Sew Creative*

Three-Dimensional Textures

No matter what you use to create 3-D images, you are limited only by your imagination in creating unique textures. Dig through your kitchen cabinets, refrigerator, hardware, sewing cabinets, and kids' toy chests, then start layering items on your scanner bed.

Locks, keys, and key chains with tissue-paper background

Shells and ribbons with lace background

Tip Scanning 3-D textures makes it easy to see whether you have everything arranged exactly as you want it. If you want to copy directly onto fabric, to save ink make test copies on plain paper in black and white in *Draft* or *Fast print* mode until you are happy with the placement of all your 3-D materials.

What You'll Need

☐ Scanner or all-in-one

☐ Clear transparency sheet

Here's How

SCANNER OR ALL-IN-ONE

1. Place a clear acetate or transparency sheet on the bed of your scanner or all-in-one to protect the glass.

2. Layer items on the bed.

3. Preview the image and adjust the objects as necessary or crop the image.

4. Scan and save the file.

Vegetables make great 3-D scans.

Try This!

☐ Try an unusual assortment of items.

Fortune-telling cards, feathers, letter tiles, and more

☐ Apply effects such as Change Colors (pages 26–27), Filters and Effects (pages 48–49), and Saturate It! (pages 18–19) to your scanned textures.

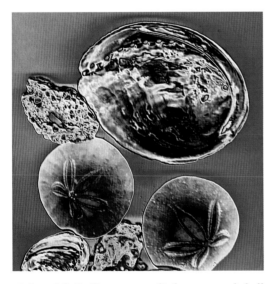

Colored foil *effect was applied to scanned shells.*

Tip Open or remove the lid of the scanner, then cover the objects with any type of fabric or paper to block the light and to create a background behind the items.

Make This!

3-D textures can be used in many ways.

Crayons and refrigerator magnets were used to create alternate blocks for this quilt of adorable Audrey.

WHAT A GIRL! *33˝ × 35˝, Lynn Koolish*

A beaded necklace was the inspiration for this gored skirt. The necklace was scanned, and the scanned image was copied and pasted multiple times in a photo-editing program to create the fabric design.

JEWELED SKIRT, *Lori Dvir-Djerassi for Color Textiles*

Banner Printing

Make your own fabric, scarves, quilt borders, or any other item (or subject) that requires a longer length of fabric.

GIRAFFE! *26˝ × 61˝, Lynn Koolish*

What You'll Need

☐ Digital images and software for printing banners

Here's How

BANNER PRINTING SOFTWARE

1. Use a software program that specifically has a *Banner* printing option.

2. Choose the *Banner* option.

3. Insert or import image files as instructed by the software.

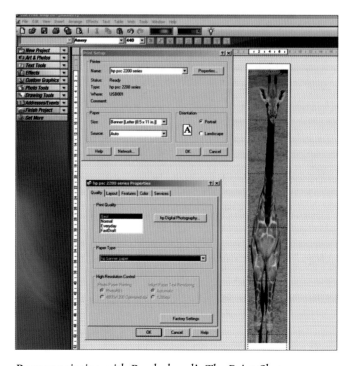

Banner printing with Broderbund's The Print Shop

4. When it's time to print, make sure your page setup is correct; for example, when printing one long photo across the length of the banner, the page setup should be *Landscape*. But, a subject such as the Eiffel Tower would be printed in *Portrait* orientation.

5. Also, be sure to use the *Print Properties* option and select *Banner* for *Paper Size* **and** *Paper Type* (see pages 6–7).

6. Do a test print on banner paper before printing on your fabric.

Tip Make sure your paper or fabric is feeding into the printer absolutely straight when printing banners.

Tip Buying pretreated fabric on rolls is a big time saver when printing banners or scarves. (See Resources on page 63.)

Try This!

☐ Combine different images into one banner and frame each image.

Outer images were mirrored to focus in on the central image.

☐ Use images that you've altered with filters, effects, or color changes.

Several leaf photos were recolored (see pages 26–27) and copied and pasted many times.

Make This!

Scarves make a personalized gift that any friend would love to receive.

A photo of a beach scene was mirrored and merged using photo-editing software, then printed out using the banner option.

COASTAL MEMORIES, *8″ × 56″, Cyndy Lyle Rymer*

Three-Dimensional Borders

Create 3-D borders around your favorite photos or scan some favorite objects and print them using the banner option (see pages 36–37) to make unique borders for quilts.

Wedding memorabilia

Layered borders

What You'll Need

☐ Scanner or all-in-one

☐ Software for printing banners (for printing long borders)

☐ Clear transparency sheet

Here's How

PHOTO BORDERS

1. Place a photo face down on the scanner or all-in-one bed, then place objects around it to create a border. If you are using items with sharp edges, place a clear acetate or transparency sheet on the bed of your scanner or all-in-one to protect the glass.

2. Preview the image and adjust the objects as necessary or crop the image. Scan.

3. Save the file, then print on fabric.

Tip Scanning makes it easy to see whether you have everything arranged exactly as you want it. If you want to copy directly onto fabric, make test copies on plain paper in black and white in *Draft* or *Fast print* mode until you are happy with the placement of your photo and border materials.

QUILT BORDERS

1. Place 3-D items on the scanner or all-in-one bed and arrange them so they will work for your quilt border. If you are using items with sharp edges, place a clear acetate or transparency sheet on the bed of your scanner or all-in-one to protect the glass.

2. Preview the image and adjust the objects as necessary or crop the image. Scan and save the file.

3. Use banner printing software to create borders in the needed lengths. You can enlarge or repeat the image as needed. (See pages 36–37 for banner printing.)

Try This!

☐ Surround a favorite photo with related items for a border. Add a second border created from more 3-D items.

 Tip For a smaller wallhanging, try placing items in two vertical rows to create borders for two sides of the quilt.

Shells lined up for quilt borders

Torn paper, a rubber-stamped title, and gardening ornaments surround garden photos for a quick gift for a gardening friend.

Make This!

Make your own border fabric for a quilt or wallhanging.

Four pages of summer memories were created using HP's Creative Scrapbook Assistant program (see pages 60–62) and Photoshop Elements. Sea glass and shells scanned on an all-in-one were used to make the 3-D border.

CAPE COD MEMORIES, 27″ × 26″, *Cyndy Lyle Rymer*

Kaleidoscopes

It doesn't matter what the subject is or whether you create them digitally or manually—kaleidoscope blocks are amazing. The easiest way to create kaleidoscopes is to use software that does all the work, but you can also make kaleidoscopes the "old-fashioned" way by cutting printed fabric using a template.

Kaleidoscope block made using HP's Creative Scrapbook Assistant

Kaleidoscope block made using Corel's Paint Shop Pro

What You'll Need

☐ Digital images and kaleidoscope software **or**

☐ Printed images and template plastic, rotary cutter, and cutting mat

Here's How

KALEIDOSCOPE SOFTWARE

We found Kaleidoscope Kreator (an inexpensive, simple program that creates kaleidoscope images in a variety of shapes and sizes) one of the *easiest* ways to create kaleidoscope images (see Resources on page 63). There's a *Quick Start Guide* in the online *Help* program, but we just clicked and experimented. It was so easy!

Star kaleidoscope

1. Open a photo file.

2. Select a shape and position the photo within the shape.

3. Preview the image and save the file.

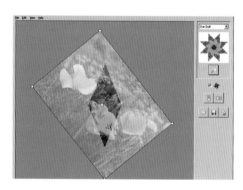

Position shape template over photo.

Tip One of the photo-editing programs we used (Paint Shop Pro) has a kaleidoscope option under the *Reflection* effect. Check your software to see what effects you have.

HAND CUT

1. Choose a photo and place it face down on the scanner or all-in-one bed.

Tip Hexagon kaleidoscopes are the easiest to make; you'll need at least 6 copies of your image for each hexagon. If you are using an all-in-one, use the option that allows you to make multiple copies.

2. Copy onto fabric (making test copies as needed).

3. Use a ruler with a 60° line to cut your triangles with a rotary cutter, or create your own template. Be sure to include ¼″ seam allowance on all sides.

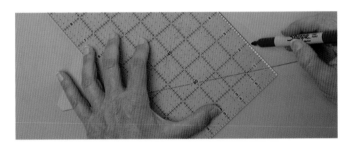

Use a ruler with a 60° line to cut template.

Tip To make sure you cut all the triangles with the exact same image, mark your template or ruler with key lines so you can line it up on the image the same way each time.

Make your own template and mark key alignment lines.

Try This!

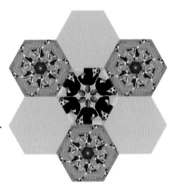

☐ Use mirror images of your file (see pages 42–43) in combination with your original photo file to create an interesting block.

☐ Combine patterned blocks with photo blocks.

Alternate three different kaleidoscope blocks.

Make This!

Create kaleidoscope blocks with 6 sides and sew them into a hexagon quilt.

FLOWER POWER, *60″×36″, Kathleen Brown for Hewlett-Packard*

Reflections and Mirrors

Enjoy a new perspective of your favorite places with mirroring and reflection. You can create an interesting composition and secondary patterns or just emphasize a favorite image by repeating it.

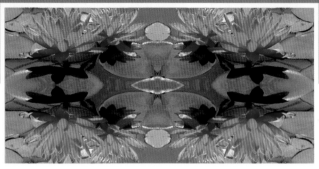

Water lilies and leaves make interesting secondary patterns.

Mirror images alternated with the original image make a mountain into an impressive mountain range.

What You'll Need

☐ Scanner, printer, or all-in-one *or*

☐ Digital images and photo-editing software

Here's How

SCANNER OR ALL-IN-ONE

1. Scan the image and save the file on your computer.

2. Preview, choose the *Mirror image* option (see page 9), and scan to a second file.

3. Print both images onto fabric and sew them together.

⁎ ─────────────────────────────

Tip When determining the size to print the images on fabric, be sure to leave ¼" for seam allowances. ⁎

PRINTER

1. Print original image on fabric.

2. Print mirror image by selecting the *Mirror image* option under *Print Properties* (see page 6).

3. Sew images together.

⁎ ─────────────────────────────

Tip You can create interesting secondary patterns if you cut or crop your image on or through one of the elements. ⁎

PHOTO-EDITING SOFTWARE

1. Open a photo file. Make a copy of the original file by saving the image under a new file name.

2. Look at your software menu options to find *Mirror* or *Flip Horizontal/Flip Vertical*. It may appear under a menu item such as *Image*, *Rotate*, or *Arrange*.

3. Depending on your software, you may find it easiest to create a new file, then *Copy* and *Paste* your original image into the new file. With some software, you may be able to work in the original file.

4. *Mirror* or *Flip* the image, then copy and paste.

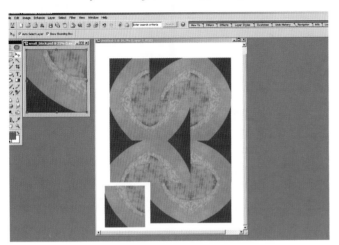

Arrange mirrored and flipped images.

5. Continue mirroring or flipping the image, copying and pasting, and arranging each image in your new file until you're happy with the result.

6. Save your new photo under the new file name.

Try This!

☐ Make a complete quilt or quilt block by flipping images and using background color.

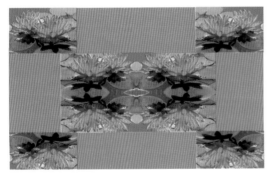

Adding a background color made the block complete.

☐ Use mirroring to design a quilt.

Make This!

One spectacular image and its mirror image make a great quilt. Mirrored images of Venice were printed and sewn together.

REFLECTIONS OF VENICE,
18˝ × 24˝, Sue Andersen for Hewlett-Packard

Panoramas

To get the "big picture," purchase a disposable panorama camera, use a camera with a panorama feature, or use software designed to stitch photos together to create panoramas.

5 photos were merged together for this panorama.

 ―――――――――――――――――――――――――――

Tip Check your camera manual to see whether your digital camera has panorama capabilities.

―――――――――――――――――――――――――――

What You'll Need

☐ Digital camera with panorama feature **or**

☐ Sequence of digital photos

☐ Panorama software

Here's How

DIGITAL CAMERA WITH BUILT-IN PANORAMA FEATURE

1. Use the camera's panorama mode to take a series of pictures. Use the internal transparent overlay to align the pictures in sequence.

2. Download the photos to your computer.

3. Use panorama software to combine the photos into one image.

PANORAMA SOFTWARE

You may be able to create panoramas with your photo-editing software, but we got the best results using software designed specifically for creating panoramas. (We used ArcSoft Panorama Maker software that came with our HP digital camera.)

1. Take a series of digital photos. Be sure to keep the camera at the same level as you shoot all the pictures.

2. Use a software program that has a *Panorama/Photomerge* option or is specifically designed just for panoramas.

3. Insert the image files as instructed by the software and follow the program instructions.

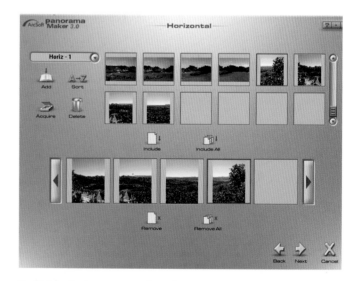

Individual photos are selected.

4. Save the file.

5. Panoramas can be printed as small or as large as you like. Some programs will walk you through printing your large image on multiple sheets that are 8½″ × 11″. Or you can bring your finished panorama image into a banner printing program (see pages 36–37) and print it on a continuous roll of fabric.

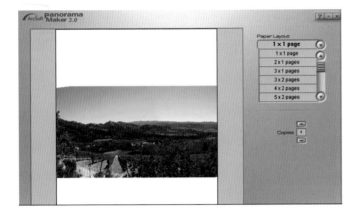

Try This!

☐ Try a complete 360° view of a scene or interior.

☐ Take pictures at a party or picnic to put into a panorama.

Tip When you take photos for panoramas, be sure the images overlap so that the software has reference points to "seam" the photos together. Digital cameras with built-in panorama capabilities have guidelines on the camera screen to help you line up your shots.

Make This!

Print your favorite panorama shot using the banner printing option, then embellish it to your heart's content.

Start with a beautiful panoramic photo, add matching fabrics to extend the borders, and embellish to create this small wallhanging. Metallic threads, beads, hand embroidery, and watercolor pencils were used to enhance the photo quilt. This is a quick and easy project completed in a day. The handwork and embellishments are an easy take-along project.

PEACEFUL VALLEY, *36″ × 24″, photos by Lynn Koolish, quilt by Barbara Baker*

Photo Montage

PhotoMontage software by ArcSoft is truly photo magic! Select photos then choose the photo file you want to use to create a central image. The software uses color filters to create the colors, shades, and tints needed to create an amazing montage of your photos.

Original photo

Photo montage

What You'll Need

☐ Digital images and PhotoMontage software by ArcSoft

Here's How

PHOTOMONTAGE SOFTWARE

1. The best way to learn how to use the program is to read the *Quick Start Tutorial* and go through the screens before starting a project.

2. Go through the screens as described in the tutorial. It's so easy, and the results are spectacular.

> **Tip** For the best image, pick a photo with one central image and edit the photo to crop out nonessential parts.

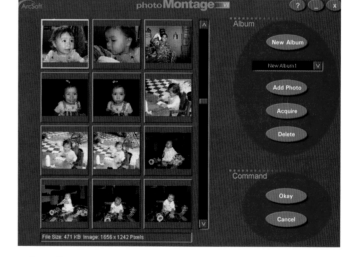

Select photo.

The more images you use for a montage, the better it looks. If you don't have a lot of photos that are related to the central image, use what you have; the final image will still look great.

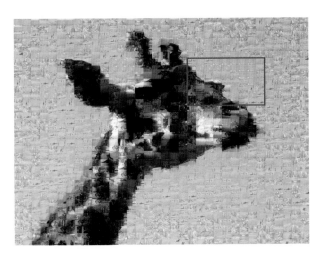

Finished giraffe montage

A wide range of photos were used to create the giraffe montage.

Try This!

☐ Take lots of photos at a birthday party or other family event, and use the photos for a photo montage quilt for the guest of honor.

☐ For a unique look, try using just 1 or 2 images to build the montage.

 ——————————————————————

Tip If you want to create a montage with a lot of photos that include one color—such as blue from a trip to a tropical resort or brown from trees at a camping site—choose a photo subject that has a lot of the desired color in it. ——————— ✳

Make This!

Vacation photos can be turned into a fabulous quilt. Select one image for the central photo montage subject and use additional photos as borders.

A photo of a villa in Tuscany was made into a photo montage, then surrounded by more photos of Tuscany.

Original photo

MEMORIES OF TUSCANY, *43˝ × 35˝*, *Cyndy Lyle Rymer*

Filters and Effects

You can achieve an amazing range of effects using the filters and effects available in photo-editing, scrapbooking, and desktop publishing software, and all you need to do is click on a button. It's that easy. Experiment with single filters and combinations. (See pages 12–13 for more information about photo-editing software and filters.)

Original photo

Wind *effect*

Poster edges *effect*

What You'll Need

☐ Digital images and photo-editing software

Here's How

PHOTO-EDITING SOFTWARE

1. Open a photo file. Make a copy of the original file by saving the image under a new file name.

2. Find the *Filters, Effects,* or *Enhance* menu. Click on it and take a look at the options.

3. Choose a filter. Many programs show you a preview of the effect on your image so you can see what the image will look like before you apply the filter. Try a few options. Some filters have options that allow you to alter the effect.

4. Save your new photo under the new file name.

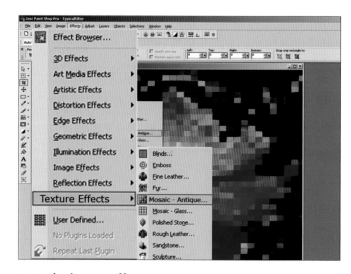

Typical Filter *or* Effect *options*

Tip If you apply a filter and decide you don't like it, use *Undo* to remove the effect.

Try This!

☐ Use multiple effects.

Original

Liquify *filter applied and the* color/hue *changed (see pages 26–27)*

A single photo of a sunset was photo montaged *(see pages 46–47),* saturation *increased (see pages 18–19), and* Twirl *filter applied*

Make This!

Use multiple filters combined with other effects to create a wide range of related images that work well together.

Original image

This fabric bowl was made from printed fabric and fast2fuse double-sided fusible stiff interfacing using a pattern from Linda Johansen's *Fast, Fun & Easy Fabric Bowls*. The original image was made into a circular shape using a *Geometric Circle* filter, then a *Color Foil* effect was applied. The hue was changed for the inner and outer sides of the bowl.

SAN DIEGO PALMS, *10˝, Lynn Koolish*

Layers and Transparency

The door to creative fabric printing opens even wider with layers and transparency. Layers allow you to stack images on top of each other. Transparency allows you to see through the layers to the images underneath.

Multiple copies of the palm leaf were layered using HP's Creative Scrapbook Assistant.

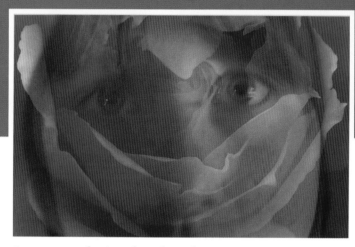

Layers created using Photoshop Elements

What You'll Need

☐ Digital images and photo-editing software *or*

☐ Creative Scrapbook Assistant

Here's How

CREATIVE SCRAPBOOK ASSISTANT

HP's Creative Scrapbook Assistant is an easy way to get started because you can stack many elements on top of each other, then adjust the transparency or opacity of each element.

(For a more complete description of Creative Scrapbook Assistant, see pages 60–62)

1. Select and drag any elements onto the page.

2. Use the *Transparency* slider to adjust the transparency of each element.

Adding layers using HP's Creative Scrapbook Assistant.

3. Control which elements appear in back of or front of others by using the following *Edit* options: *Move Forward, Move Backward, Move to Back, Move to Front.*

PHOTO-EDITING SOFTWARE

Using layers in photo-editing software can be a challenge at first, but once you learn your way around your program you'll be using layers all the time. Each program is different, so your best bet is to find the tutorial or *Help* files for your program and use them to learn how layers work.

You can control the opacity of each layer as well as the order in which the layers appear.

Tip For an easy way to layer two images without using software, print or copy one of the images onto inkjet transparency film (available at most office supply stores). Lay the transparency film on top of a printed photo and place both on the bed of a scanner or all-in-one. Then scan or copy directly to fabric.

Original photo and leaf printed on HP transparency film

Overlay transparency, then copy or scan.

Try This!

☐ Use 2 images (each in its own layer) and vary the transparency or opacity of each layer to see the effect.

The cruise ship was layered over Denali using Photoshop Elements.

Make This!

IT'S ALWAYS TIME TO SEW, *8″, Lynn Koolish*

This clock was made from printed fabric and 2 layers of fast2fuse double-sided fusible stiff interfacing. Using layers in Photoshop made it easy to precisely place the images (spools of thread and buttons), which otherwise rolled and got out of place.

GARDEN ANGEL, *7″ × 9″, Cyndy Lyle Rymer*

Several photos were layered and the level of transparency adjusted for each using photo-editing software. The layered photo was made into a small wallhanging using fast2fuse double-sided fusible stiff interfacing.

Move It Fun-House Mirrors

Moving an item while scanning—whether it's a photo or an object—is a fascinating experiment. Try moving things in different directions for a variety of fun-house effects! You can also use Filters and Effects (see pages 48–49) for similar results.

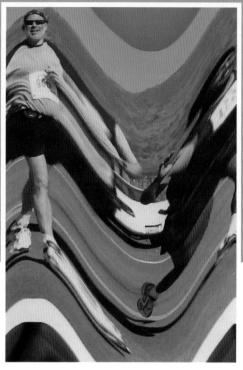

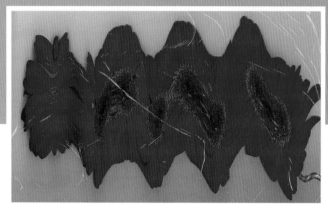

Flowers with plastic wrap to protect the scanner bed; the plastic wrap provided additional texture

Photo of runners moved during scanning

What You'll Need

- ☐ Scanner or all-in-one **or**
- ☐ Digital images and photo-editing software

Here's How

SCANNER OR ALL-IN-ONE

1. Choose a photo or object to scan or copy. You can attach your photo or 3-D item to a bamboo skewer or a wire to make moving it while scanning (or copying) easier and to keep your hands out of the way.

Tape a wire to the back of the photo.

2. Move the photo or object while scanning. Try moving it horizontally, vertically, or in circles or curves while scanning.

Keep the lid open for a dark background.

 ———————————————————

Tip For a light-colored background, lift the lid of the scanner or all-in-one slightly; for a dark-colored background, open the lid entirely or remove it.

———————————————————

3. Keep in mind that there are usually two phases to scanning—previewing and accepting. When accepting, the image is actually rescanned, so for this effect, what you see in the preview is not what you'll get as the final scan. You will need to repeat your movements for the "real" scan.

Tip Scanning and saving your image to a computer allows you to make sure you have the image you want. If you want to copy and print directly on fabric, you won't know the final result until it is actually printed.

PHOTO-EDITING SOFTWARE

Use the software Help tool, Quick Start, Hints, or Recipes as necessary.

1. Open a photo file. Make a copy of the original file by saving the image under a new file name.

2. Find the *Filters, Effects,* or *Enhance* menu. Click on it and look for *Liquify* and *Twirl.*

3. Experiment with both to see what effects you can get.

4. Save your new photo under the new file name.

Original photo

Liquify *filter applied*

Twirl *filter applied*

Try This!

☐ Move a photo in various ways for fun-house mirror effects.

☐ Move a collaged image in various ways as the scanner lamp moves.

Move photo in a slow zigzag.

Move printed image in steps as the scanner lamp moves.

Make This!

Photo-editing software filters proved lots of fun for fun house mirror effects. Made using Photoshop Elements and the *Distort* filter, this little wallhanging was made using fast2fuse double-sided fusible stiff interfacing as the batting.

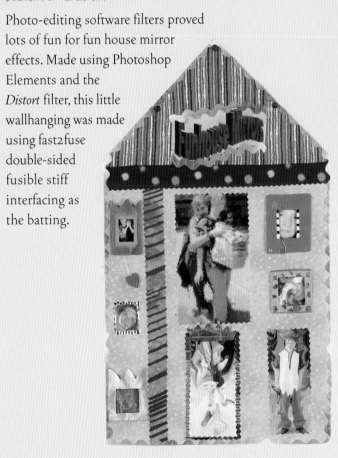

FUNHOUSE MIRRORS, *14˝ × 18˝, Cyndy Lyle Rymer*

Photo Transfer

When you want to use an image and can't print it on fabric first or you want to create an effect that can't easily be done by printing directly on fabric, use photo transfer! It's also an alternative to traditional appliqué.

Original image (from The Vintage Workshop; *see Resources on page 63)*

Reversed for photo transfer

What You'll Need

☐ Printer, scanner, or all-in-one

☐ Photo prints or digital images

☐ Photo transfer paper

Here's How

PRINTER, SCANNER, OR ALL-IN-ONE

1. Print or copy your image onto the photo transfer paper. Note: The image needs to be printed in reverse so that when it is ironed on it will be correct. When printing, use *Print Properties* (see pages 6–7) to set the *Paper* setting to

Iron-on Transfer or use a *mirror image* option. Similar options are available when copying is done using an all-in-one.

2. Cut out the printed image.

3. For a soft, antique-looking edge, you can use sandpaper to lightly sand the edges.

4. Follow the manufacturer's instructions to iron the image onto fabric.

Tip For best results when ironing, do not use steam and use a very firm ironing surface. An ironing board is too soft to allow the image to transfer completely.

Try This!

☐ Make multiple copies of the same image and overlap to create an image collage.

☐ Use small images to add decorative touches to premade garments that would be difficult to stitch on.

✳ ─────────────────────────────

Tip Protect the first layer with tissue paper when transferring multiple layers.

─────────────────────────── ✳

Photo transfer applied to a denim jacket allows the fabric to show through and add color and texture to the image.

Make This!

Photo transfers can be used for all sorts of fun projects.

A treasure map was printed on photo transfer paper. The edges were sanded, then the map was folded and the creases sanded to create a weathered look.

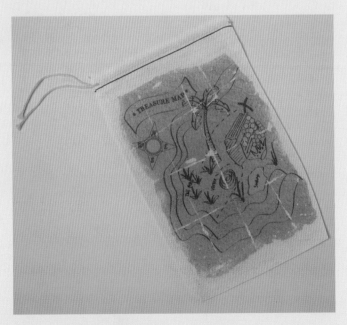

TREASURE MAP PARTY FAVOR BAGS,
4″ × 6″, Lynn Koolish

More Than a Label

The Hewlett-Packard Custom Label Kit is not just for quilt labels, although you can make great original labels with it. You can create custom appliqués, quilt blocks, and small quilts or even create your own fabric.

Photo Log Cabin block

Quick and easy framed image

To make the Custom Label Kit software even better, you can update it by logging on to the HP website (see resources on page 63) and use the search box to look for "Expanding your quilt label kit." You'll be able to download new templates and clip art for even more possibilities.

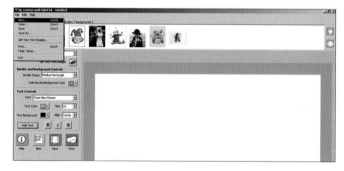

Start with a blank page.

What You'll Need

☐ Custom Label Kit from Hewlett-Packard and digital images or images that come with the software

☐ Access to the web (optional, for updates)

Here's How

The best way to begin is to use *Getting Started* from the online *Help*. It will walk you through everything you need to know to start a project.

Add a background, an image, and a frame.

Try This!

☐ Put a frame or border around an image, add text, and make a pillow or small wallhanging.

☐ Use the built-in images and lettering to make soft sculpture blocks or a mobile.

HAPPY ANNIVERSARY, *6″ × 8″, Hewlett-Packard staff*

FOREST ALPHABET BLOCKS, *3″ × 3″ × 3″, Lynn Koolish*

Make This!

HEARTS, *14″ × 40″, Hewlett-Packard staff*

Use the HP Custom Label Kit to print blocks for a quilt or wallhanging. The program makes it easy to combine text and images.

These little drawstring bags are easy to make and embroider. Embroidery designs by Oklahoma Embroidery Supply & Design; drawstring bag provided by All About Blanks (see Resources on page 63).

PRINTED BAGS, *11″ × 15″, Gloria Borschowa*

Embellishing

Anything goes when it comes to embellishing your printed fabric. You can embroider (by hand or machine); embellish with trapunto; or add 3-D shapes or appliqués, buttons, beads, and more. You're limited only by your imagination.

Embroidery is the perfect embellishment for printed images. Embroidered by Gloria Borschowa. Embroidery designs by Oklahoma Embroidery Supply & Design; pillow, bib, and blanket provided by All About Blanks (see Resources on page 63).

Trapunto enhances the billowing sails.
INTO THE WIND, 16″ × 16″, Kathleen Brown for Hewlett-Packard

Make This!

☐ Use your machine's decorative stitches and embroidery.

Embroidery designs by Marcia Pollard were machine embroidered on this adorable tote bag around and on top of the printed images.

MESH TOTE BAG, 16″ × 15″ × 3″, Jennifer Nobile for Pollard's Sew Creative

BABY PILLOWS, 10″ × 7″ and 16″ × 11″, Hewlett-Packard staff, embroidery by Gloria Borschowa

Embroidery designs by Oklahoma Embroidery Supply & Design; pillows provided by All About Blanks (see Resources on page 63).

☐ Sew or glue keepsakes and mementos to a scrapbook-
   style quilt.

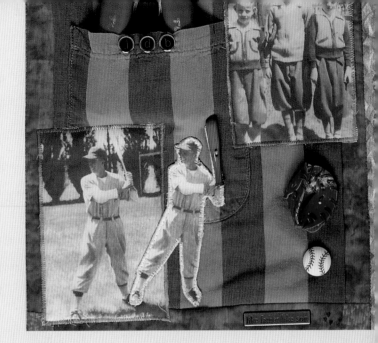

GANANOQUE DAYS, *26˝ × 28˝, Cyndy Lyle Rymer*

Beads, buttons, and fishing paraphernalia, decorate this
father-and-son fishing quilt.

PAPPA AT BAT, *14˝ × 18˝, Amy Marson*

IN THE GARDEN, *24˝ × 24˝, Hewlett-Packard staff*

A photo of tulips was printed poster size (see pages
32–33 for poster printing) and garden-themed embellishments were printed, cut out, and faced so they could be
loosely tacked to the quilt to add dimension and color.

Photos on fabric fused to fast2fuse double-sided
fusible stiff interfacing and miniature bats, balls,
and mitts embellish this scrapbook quilt.

Creative Scrapbooking

Creative Scrapbook Assistant is a gift for scrapbookers *and* quilters. Combine text with images, create custom elements such as shapes and embellishments, use photos to create frames and backgrounds, and make your own fabric. Layers and transparency are a snap.

Scrapbook pages made using HP's Creative Scrapbook Assistant

What You'll Need

☐ Digital images and Creative Scrapbook Assistant software by Hewlett-Packard

Here's How

The best way to begin is to use *Getting Started* from the online *Help*. It will walk you through everything you need to know to start a project.

Try This!

☐ Use a predesigned layout for a quick an easy page.

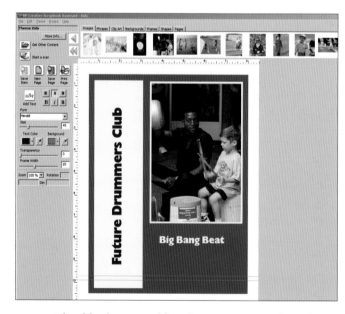

Start with a blank page. Add a photo, caption, and a title.

☐ Create your own layered backgrounds.

☐ Use filters (see pages 48–49) to create your own background.

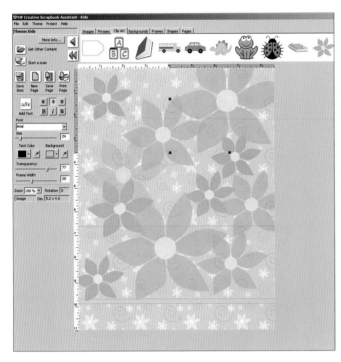

Start with a solid background and add motifs.

The Colored foil *filter was applied to a photo for the background, then photos were placed in the circle shapes to look like portholes.*

☐ Use shapes and frames to feature photos.

Layer photos and text on top.

Graphic shapes add fun and variety.

☐ Use the shape tool, borders, and clip art to make scrapbook pages.

Make a scrapbook quilt or tote bag using your favorite
photos and Creative Scrapbook Assistant.

WEDDING RING TOTE BAG, *16˝ × 20˝*,
Katrina Hamer for Hewlett-Packard

Photo Shapes by Quiltsmart (an add-on option to
the Creative Scrapbooking Assistant— see Resources
on page 63) was used to create the easiest double
wedding ring!

Resources

Please note that some of the resources listed below are wholesale manufacturers and sell to the public only through retail stores; others sell from their websites. The listed websites are often invaluable resources for projects, tips, and other information.

Hewlett-Packard Company
Printers, all-in-ones, digital cameras, software, photo transfer paper, photo printing paper, banner printing paper
www.hp.com/go/quilting/book

Adobe
Photo-editing and other software
www.adobe.com

All About Blanks
Linens and blanks for embroidery and embellishing
www.allaboutblanks.com

ArcSoft
Panorama Maker, PhotoMontage, and other software
www.arcsoft.com

Blumenthal Lansing
Pretreated fabric sheets and images and projects on CD
www.blumenthallansing.com

Broderbund
Desktop publishing and other software
800-395-0277
www.broderbund.com

C. Jenkins Necktie & Chemical Company
Bubble Jet Set 2000 and Rinse, freezer paper sheets, and pretreated fabric sheets
314-521-7544
www.cjenkinscompany.com

Color Textiles
Pretreated fabric sheets and rolls and kits
702-838-5868
www.colortextiles.com

Corel
Photo-editing and other software
www.corel.com

Electric Quilt
Software and pretreated fabric sheets
www.electricquilt.com

fast2fuse
C&T Publishing
1-800-284-1114
www.ctpub.com

Jacquard
Pretreated fabric sheets, fabric paints and other supplies
800-442-0455
www.jacquardproducts.com

June Tailor
Pretreated fabric sheets, photo transfer paper, and notions
800-844-5400
www.junetailor.com

Kaleidoscope Collections
Kaleidoscope Kreator software
www.kaleidoscopecollections.com

Oklahoma Embroidery Supply & Design
Embroidery designs and supplies
www.embroideryonline.com

Printed Treasures
Pretreated fabric sheets
www.printedtreasures.com

Quiltsmart
Double Wedding Ring and other add-on shapes for HP Creative Scrapbooking program
www.quiltsmart.com

The Vintage Workshop
Pretreated fabric sheets and images and projects on CD
913-648-2700
www.thevintageworkshop.com

Quilting Supplies
Cotton Patch Mail Order
3404 Hall Lane
Dept. CTB
Lafayette, CA 94549
800-835-4418/925-283-7883
email: quiltusa@yahoo.com
website: www.quiltusa.com

For More Information about other books by C&T Publishing
Ask for a free catalog:
C&T Publishing, Inc.
P.O. Box 1456
Lafayette, CA 94549
800-284-1114
email: ctinfo@ctpub.com
website: www.ctpub.com

About the Authors

Cyndy Lyle Rymer and Lynn Koolish are developmental editors at C&T Publishing. Both are enthusiastic digital photographers, software explorers, and avid quilters. Working together on this book gave them the opportunity for collaborative creativity and fabric adventures.

Hewlett-Packard is a world leader in printing and imaging and has dedicated an entire team to helping quilters learn how to use technology products in their craft. By providing hardware and software solutions designed by quilters for quilters, HP is helping make this exciting new aspect of quilting come to life. No worries, no complicated instructions or hard-to-understand technology— HP's offerings of cameras, printers, scanners, and software and its exciting website all make it easy. More than ever, it is fun and exciting to capture memories and express yourself in quilting, adding that special, personalized touch. Visit HP's quilting website at www.hp.com/go/quilting/book for all the latest projects, tips, and inspiration.

Index